C000120828

The
Amazing
Cross

The Amazing Cross

Transforming Lives Today

**6 STUDIES FOR INDIVIDUALS
OR SMALL GROUPS**

Elizabeth McQuoid

INTER-VARSITY PRESS
Norton Street, London SW1P 4ST, England
Email: ivp@ivpbooks.com
Website: www.ivpbooks.com

© Elizabeth McQuoid, 2016

Elizabeth McQuoid has asserted her right under the Copyright, Designs and Patents Act
1988 to be identified as Author of this work. All rights reserved. No part of this publication
may be reproduced, stored in a retrieval system, or transmitted, in any form or by any
means, electronic, mechanical, photocopying, recording or otherwise, without the prior
permission of the publisher or the Copyright Licensing Agency.

Unless otherwise stated, Scripture quotations are taken from the Holy Bible, New
International Version® Anglicized, NIV® Copyright © 1979, 1984, 2011 by Biblica, Inc.®
Used by permission. All rights reserved worldwide.

Scripture quotations marked *The Message* are from *The Message*. Copyright © 1993, 1994,
1995, 1996, 2000, 2001, 2002. Used by permission of NavPress Publishing Group.

First published 2016

British Library Cataloguing in Publication Data
A catalogue record for this book is available from the British Library.

ISBN: 978–1–78359–418–4

Set in Warnock
Typeset in Great Britain by CRB Associates, Potterhanworth, Lincolnshire
Printed and bound in Great Britain by Ashford Colour Press Ltd, Gosport, Hampshire

*Inter-Varsity Press publishes Christian books that are true to the Bible and that
communicate the gospel, develop discipleship and strengthen the church for its mission
in the world.*

*IVP originated within the Inter-Varsity Fellowship, now the Universities and Colleges
Christian Fellowship, a student movement connecting Christian Unions in universities and
colleges throughout Great Britain, and a member movement of the International Fellowship
of Evangelical Students. Website: www.uccf.org.uk. That historic association is maintained,
and all senior IVP staff and committee members subscribe to the UCCF Basis of Faith.*

Contents

Introduction

It stands at the crossroads of history – literally dividing time into a 'before' and an 'after'.

Words like 'monumental' and 'pivotal' are totally inadequate to describe the impact that the cross of Christ has had on the history of the world. Nothing would ever be the same again.

The cross can't be ignored. It demands a response, because the man who hung there claimed to be God. Many thought he was deluded, but others, who witnessed his death and resurrection, willingly gave their lives because they believed his message.

And so, with the cross at its centre, the gospel message lives on.

The cross stands as a stake in the ground demonstrating to every generation God's amazing love and grace. It was the culmination of the Trinity's plans from before the dawn of time: Christ dying in our place, the once-and-for-all payment for sin, dealing the fatal blow to Satan and defeating death forever.

The earth shook as the wrath of God was poured out on Christ's body. Darkness covered the land when God could no longer look on his darling Son. The curtain of the temple, which separated people from God, was torn in two, and Jesus cried, 'It is finished.'

The way to God was opened up for all. But it was costly. The agony Jesus experienced at Calvary and the anguish the Father felt in sending him to die are unimaginable. And yet their pain offers us comfort and hope. The cross declares that God does not stand remote and aloof from our suffering – he joins us in it.

And for those of us who would be Christ's disciples, the cross sets our daily course; it is the road we must travel. Following the way of the cross is a constant challenge to 'put to death' our own agendas and desires, and put Christ – his values, priorities and will – at the centre of our lives.

There's a wonderful story about the great French sculptor Auguste Rodin, who one day saw a huge, carved crucifix beside a road. He found the sculpture so moving that he purchased it and arranged to have the cross carted back to his house. But, unfortunately, it was too big for the building. So, what did he do? He knocked out the walls, raised the roof and rebuilt his home around the cross.

Our hope is that this study will help us rebuild our lives round the cross.

The passion of the cross

▶ INTRODUCTION

We daren't admit it, but sometimes we get so familiar with the gospel and the crucifixion scene that we lose our sense of awe. To recapture the passion behind the events of Good Friday, we need to understand the love that existed in the Trinity before the dawn of time: each member of the Godhead loving one other perfectly, selflessly, endlessly. Imagine, then, the anguish of God the Father sending his only Son to die and what it cost the Son to obey. This is the price they willingly paid, because they knew there was no other remedy for sin. The cross displays the perfect love within the Godhead. Only there can we truly see, for all of time and eternity, how much God loves us.

READ *Romans 5:1-8*

Therefore, since we have been justified through faith, we have peace with God through our Lord Jesus Christ, [2] through whom we have gained access by faith into this grace in which we now stand. And we boast in the hope of the glory of God. [3] Not only so, but we also glory in our sufferings, because we know that suffering produces perseverance; [4] perseverance, character; and character, hope. [5] And hope does not put us to shame, because God's love has been poured out into our hearts through the Holy Spirit, who has been given to us.

[6] You see, at just the right time, when we were still powerless, Christ died for the ungodly. [7] Very rarely will anyone die for a righteous person, though for a good person someone might possibly dare to die. [8] But God demonstrates his own love for us in this: while we were still sinners, Christ died for us.

 FOCUS ON THE THEME

1.   Why do we often doubt God's love?

 WHAT DOES THE BIBLE SAY?

2.   How has God demonstrated his love for us? Look at verses 5 and 8.

3. Why is the cross such a surprising demonstration of God's love? See verses 6–8.

It has been said that 'something is worth what someone else is willing to pay.' Christ's willingness to give his life shows the value he placed on me.

(*The Amazing Cross*, p. 26)

4. What difference does it make that we have God's love in our hearts (verses 2b–5)?

5. According to this passage, to what extent are our circumstances an indicator of how much God loves us?

The Christian Gospel is that I am so flawed that Jesus had to die for me, yet I am so loved and valued that Jesus was glad to die for me.

(Timothy Keller, *The Reason for God: Belief in an Age of Scepticism*, p. 179)

⊙ INVESTIGATE FURTHER

6. Christ's death on the cross was the supreme demonstration of how much God loves us. However, God shows his love daily in many ways. Look up some examples:
    - Psalm 23:1–4

- Matthew 5:43–45

- Romans 8:34

- Hebrews 12:5–6

♥ LIVING IT OUT

7. Think about Jesus' life on earth. In what practical ways did he demonstrate his love for his Father? How can we imitate him?

8. Consider the love God the Father and Son displayed at the cross. How can we show this type of self-giving love in our closest relationships? Think about the love you show to your:
   - Parents

   - Children

   - Spouse

9. Imagine the following conversations. How would you respond?
   - Your Christian friend is going through a difficult time and says, 'I don't think God really loves me.'

- A work colleague says, 'Look at all the evil in the world – a God of love wouldn't allow these things to happen.'

- A mother at the school gate says, 'I couldn't love a God who killed his own son: that's barbaric.'

10. What difference would it make to your thoughts and behaviour if you were more aware of God's love for you? How could you remind yourself daily of God's love? Think about practical steps you could take.

You may often feel like giving up [serving God]. You may face opposition and hostility, discouragement and setbacks . . . What do you do when these things happen? We need to go sunbathing! We need to put ourselves again in the sunshine of God's love . . . We live in a cold, graceless world. But when we step into the warmth of God's love, our cold hearts are warmed and our weary souls are energized.

(Tim Chester, *Mission Matters*, p. 24)

▲ PRAYER TIME

Gaze into the mystery. Remind yourself of the cost of your salvation. What the Father and Son went through 'together' to know you and be known by you.

(*The Amazing Cross*, p. 35).

My response is to get down on my knees before the Father, this magnificent Father who parcels out all heaven and earth. I ask him to strengthen you by his Spirit – not a brute strength but a glorious inner strength – that Christ will live in you as you open the door and invite him in. And I ask him that with both feet planted firmly on love, you'll be able to take in with all followers of Jesus the extravagant dimensions of Christ's love. Reach out and experience the breadth! Test its length! Plumb the depths! Rise to the heights! Live full lives, full in the fullness of God.

(Ephesians 3:14–19, *The Message*)

 # FURTHER STUDY

Below is a selection of books to help you reflect more on God's love and the impact it has on our lives:

D. A. Carson and Kathleen B. Nielson, *God's Love Compels Us: Taking the Gospel to the World* (Crossway, 2015)

Francis Chan, *Crazy Love: Overwhelmed by a Relentless God* (Kingsway, 2009)

Ajith Fernando, *Reclaiming Love: Radical Relationships in a Complex World* (Zondervan, 2013)

John Ortberg, *Love beyond Reason: Moving God's Love from Your Head to Your Heart* (Zondervan, 2001)

The perfect storm

▶ INTRODUCTION

We don't like to think of God as a God of wrath. It doesn't fit with our understanding of God's love and it clashes with our storybook image of 'gentle Jesus, meek and mild', children clambering on his lap. It's uncomfortable to think about God's hatred of sin and his divine anger that needs to be appeased. But the cross was actually a demonstration of God's amazing love; it was there my punishment was dealt with. At the cross God's wrath was satisfied because Jesus took my place. All our sin – past, present and future – was laid on him. So what happens now? Surely Jesus' sacrifice urges us to hate sin as much as God does and to strive to be holy!

READ *Isaiah 53:4-10*

⁴*Surely he took up our pain*
    and bore our suffering,
yet we considered him punished by God,
    stricken by him, and afflicted.
⁵*But he was pierced for our transgressions,*
    he was crushed for our iniquities;
the punishment that brought us peace was on him,
    and by his wounds we are healed.
⁶*We all, like sheep, have gone astray,*
    each of us has turned to our own way;
and the LORD has laid on him
    the iniquity of us all.
⁷*He was oppressed and afflicted,*
    yet he did not open his mouth;
he was led like a lamb to the slaughter,
    and as a sheep before its shearers is silent,
    so he did not open his mouth.
⁸*By oppression and judgment he was taken away.*
    Yet who of his generation protested?
For he was cut off from the land of the living;
    for the transgression of my people he was punished.
⁹*He was assigned a grave with the wicked,*
    and with the rich in his death,
though he had done no violence,
    nor was any deceit in his mouth.
¹⁰*Yet it was the LORD's will to crush him and cause him to suffer,*
    and though the LORD makes his life an offering for sin,
he will see his offspring and prolong his days,
    and the will of the LORD will prosper in his hand.

⊙ FOCUS ON THE THEME

1. Why do we struggle to think of God as a God of wrath?

God does not get angry like we do. His wrath is not the irrational outburst of an unbalanced temper. Quite the opposite, God's wrath is the consistent response of his holy character to any and every shade of sin. As John Stott puts it in his Romans commentary, 'his wrath is his holy hostility to evil, his refusal to condone or come to terms with it, his just judgment upon it.'

(*The Amazing Cross*, p. 46; John Stott quoting from *The Message of Romans*, p. 72)

● WHAT DOES THE BIBLE SAY?

2. What image does verse 6 use to describe us? How does it help us understand what sin is?

3. Look through Isaiah 53:4–10. Pick out the phrases that describe Jesus:

    • Facing God's wrath

    • Taking our punishment

4. How do these verses convey God's hatred of sin?

5. Isaiah wrote these words about 700 years before Jesus' crucifixion. Why do you think God gave Isaiah this prophecy and what does it tell us about God's salvation plan?

Here is the glory of the cross. God, in his amazing grace, has dealt with his own holy hatred of sin in a way that rescues us from horrendous judgment. God chose to pour out his wrath on Jesus instead of us. And Christ was willing to pay that awful price.

(*The Amazing Cross*, p. 46)

◉ INVESTIGATE FURTHER

6. Why was Jesus able to appease God's wrath? What made him the perfect sacrifice? Look at Hebrews 7:26–28.

7. We've escaped God's wrath, but we still have to face his judgment. What does this mean for a believer? Look at:

    • 2 Corinthians 5:10

    • 1 Corinthians 3:12–15

♥ LIVING IT OUT

8.   Imagine what you would say in the following conversations:

- A Christian friend says, 'Surely there are different shades of sin? God can't judge all sin the same.'

- A group member at an Alpha/Christianity Explored course comments, 'I've lived a good life, better than most. I'm sure God will accept me into heaven.'

If we cannot see how ugly, how death-dealing, how God-defying sin is, we shall not see how utterly satisfying the cross is, by which men and women alone are reconciled to God.

(D. A. Carson, quoted in *The Amazing Cross*, p. 42)

9.   Although we know that we have been forgiven, some of us still feel guilty because of past sins and failures.

- What are the tell-tale signs that we are living with guilt?

- How can we get rid of guilt?

10.   Reflect on the passages you've read and the issues raised in this study. As you live for God this week, what will motivate you? What have you learnt today that will spur you on?

▲ PRAYER TIME

Spend time in silence confessing your sins to God. Together, thank God for his forgiveness and the freedom from guilt that we can enjoy. Pray for one another – that with the Holy Spirit's help we would live lives that please God.

● FURTHER STUDY

The doctrine theologians call 'penal substitution' – that Jesus stood in our place and appeased God's wrath – has been fiercely debated in recent years. If you would like to look into the background and meaning behind this idea of propitiation/atonement, use a Bible dictionary or visit a website such as biblegateway.com to do a word search. You could also read Brian Edwards and Ian Shaw, *The Divine Substitute: The Atonement in the Bible and History* (Day One Publications, 2006), or Steve Jeffery, Mike Ovey and Andrew Sach, *Pierced for Our Transgressions: Rediscovering the Glory of Penal Substitution* (IVP, 2007).

Justification: A righteousness from God

▶ **INTRODUCTION**

Often we look at our work colleagues or even friends at church, and we compare ourselves quite favourably. So we rest on our laurels and feel satisfied that we are good enough. It is only when we compare ourselves to the white-hot holiness of God that we realize the extent of our sin. As Paul explains in Romans, even the very best of us are sinners, and there is nothing we can do to save ourselves from God's punishment. But at Calvary the charges against us were dropped when Jesus paid the penalty for our sin in full. The good news of the gospel is that on the cross Jesus took our sin and, as an act of sheer grace, gives us his righteousness, so that we can stand justified before God.

READ *Romans 3:9-26*

What shall we conclude then? Do we have any advantage? Not at all! For we have already made the charge that Jews and Gentiles alike are all under the power of sin. [10]*As it is written:*

> *'There is no one righteous, not even one;*
> [11]   *there is no one who understands;*
>   *there is no one who seeks God.*
> [12]*All have turned away,*
>   *they have together become worthless;*
> *there is no one who does good,*
>   *not even one.'*
> [13]*'Their throats are open graves;*
>   *their tongues practise deceit.'*
> *'The poison of vipers is on their lips.'*
> [14]   *'Their mouths are full of cursing and bitterness.'*
> [15]*'Their feet are swift to shed blood;*
> [16]   *ruin and misery mark their ways,*
> [17]*and the way of peace they do not know.'*
> [18]   *'There is no fear of God before their eyes.'*

[19]*Now we know that whatever the law says, it says to those who are under the law, so that every mouth may be silenced and the whole world held accountable to God.* [20]*Therefore no one will be declared righteous in God's sight by the works of the law; rather, through the law we become conscious of our sin.*

[21]*But now apart from the law the righteousness of God has been made known, to which the Law and the Prophets testify.* [22]*This righteousness is given through faith in Jesus Christ to all who believe. There is no difference between Jew and Gentile,* [23]*for all have sinned and fall short of the glory of God,* [24]*and all are justified freely by his grace through the redemption that came by Christ Jesus.* [25]*God presented Christ as a sacrifice of atonement through the shedding of his blood – to be received by faith. He did this to demonstrate his righteousness, because in his forbearance he had left the sins committed beforehand unpunished* [26] *– he did it to demonstrate his righteousness at the present time, so as to be just and the one who justifies those who have faith in Jesus.*

⟳ FOCUS ON THE THEME

1. Think back to a time when someone showed you grace, some kindness you didn't deserve. What happened? How did you feel?

○ WHAT DOES THE BIBLE SAY?

2. How many times is the word 'no' repeated in verses 9–20, and the word 'all' repeated in verses 22–24? What point is Paul making?

3. Look at verses 20–25:

   - What did Jesus do to justify us?

   - What do we receive from God when we are justified?

   - What do we have to do to be justified?

Is it my obedience, consecration, and dedication that make me right with God? It is never that! I am made right with God because, prior to all of that, Christ died. When I turn to God and by belief accept what God reveals, the miraculous atonement by the Cross of Christ instantly places me into a right relationship with God. And as a result of the supernatural miracle of God's grace I stand justified, not because I am sorry for my sin, or because I have repented, but because of what Jesus has done. The Spirit

*of God brings justification with a shattering, radiant light, and I know that
I am saved, even though I don't know how it was accomplished.*

(Oswald Chambers, *My Utmost for His Highest*)

4. According to these verses, how is our justification affected by:

    - Good works we do before becoming a Christian?

    - Sins we commit after becoming a Christian?

5. What does God's desire 'to be just and the one who justifies' tell us
    about his character (verses 25–26)?

◎ INVESTIGATE FURTHER

6. What are the results of our justification (see Romans 5:1–2)?

7. What difference did being justified make to Paul's daily life? Look at
    Philippians 3:7–11.

♥ LIVING IT OUT

8.   Imagine what you would say in the following scenarios:

   - A new Christian who said, 'I'm worried that I'm not really a Christian. I don't feel any different. I don't feel saved.'

   - A work colleague who said, 'I couldn't follow a God who forgives murderers, child abusers or rapists.'

   - A Christian facing difficulties who says, 'I wonder whether God is punishing me for past sins.'

Satan comes, in our imaginations, into the courtroom, and he says to the Father, 'Look at that sinner, how can you declare him justified?' 'Well, yes,' says the Father, 'they are a sinner. The charges that you bring are valid, but will you look at my Son's hands? And look at my Son's feet? And will you look at the wounds in my Son's side? Who are you to condemn? It is Christ who justifies.'

(Alistair Begg, quoted in *The Amazing Cross*, p. 75)

9.   What difference does it make that justification is based not on our emotions or performance, but on Christ's perfect sacrifice on the cross?

10. Justification is an act of God's grace. Think of ways you could share God's grace with someone this week.

▲ PRAYER TIME

Christians of past generations often talked about being 'trophies of God's grace'. Imagine each one of us as trophies in God's display case – proof of his victory over Satan and the justification he won for us, on display for all eternity, reminding everyone of his goodness and grace.

Thank God for the grace he has shown us – not only at Calvary, but daily. Pray for specific situations – at work, in the family, in our church and community – where we can be grace-givers.

⬤ FURTHER STUDY

Read through Romans 3 – 5 and trace Paul's argument about justification. What are the key words and phrases? What are Paul's main points? What new things have you learnt, or what has God reminded you about from these verses? What difference will these truths make to your life?

Redemption: Set free to become what we are

▶ INTRODUCTION

When children are asleep, they are pictures of angelic innocence. But they aren't awake for very long before we are confronted with reality! And it is not just our children; our own hearts confirm the stark truth that from birth each of us was a sinner. We are in fact slaves to sin. The Bible tells us that we need a redeemer – someone to pay the ransom price and set us free from sin. On the cross, Jesus' blood paid that ransom price once and for all. We are now free: not free to do what we want, but free to become what we are – slaves to God.

READ *Hebrews 9:11-15, 24-28*

¹¹*But when Christ came as high priest of the good things that are now already here, he went through the greater and more perfect tabernacle that is not made with human hands, that is to say, is not a part of this creation.* ¹²*He did not enter by means of the blood of goats and calves; but he entered the Most Holy Place once for all by his own blood, so obtaining eternal redemption.* ¹³*The blood of goats and bulls and the ashes of a heifer sprinkled on those who are ceremonially unclean sanctify them so that they are outwardly clean.* ¹⁴*How much more, then, will the blood of Christ, who through the eternal Spirit offered himself unblemished to God, cleanse our consciences from acts that lead to death, so that we may serve the living God!*

¹⁵*For this reason Christ is the mediator of a new covenant, that those who are called may receive the promised eternal inheritance – now that he has died as a ransom to set them free from the sins committed under the first covenant.*

²⁴*For Christ did not enter a sanctuary made with human hands that was only a copy of the true one; he entered heaven itself, now to appear for us in God's presence.* ²⁵*Nor did he enter heaven to offer himself again and again, the way the high priest enters the Most Holy Place every year with blood that is not his own.* ²⁶*Otherwise Christ would have had to suffer many times since the creation of the world. But he has appeared once for all at the culmination of the ages to do away with sin by the sacrifice of himself.* ²⁷*Just as people are destined to die once, and after that to face judgment,* ²⁸*so Christ was sacrificed once to take away the sins of many; and he will appear a second time, not to bear sin, but to bring salvation to those who are waiting for him.*

FOCUS ON THE THEME

1. Society says that we are born basically good, but the Bible says that we are born slaves to sin. Does our morality at birth really matter?

Q WHAT DOES THE BIBLE SAY?

2. What does Hebrews 9:12–14 teach us about why Jesus could redeem us and why animal sacrifices couldn't?

3. What are the results of Jesus' redemption? Look at verses 14–15.

4. Why is Jesus' sacrifice better than that of the other high priests? Look at verses 25–28.

5. According to verses 24 and 28, what is Jesus doing now?

◉ INVESTIGATE FURTHER

6. Read Romans 6:16–18. Describe the change that happened when we were redeemed.

7. Redemption means we are free from the penalty of sin, but we still feel its influence. How does Paul say we should resist sin? See Romans 6:11–14.

You and I need to be talking to ourselves, and saying, 'But don't you know that you are one with Christ; that you have died to sin, and risen to God? Don't you know that you are a slave to God, and committed therefore to obedience? Don't you know these things?' And go on asking yourself that question until you reply to yourself, 'Yes I do know. And by the grace of God I shall live accordingly.'

(John Stott, in *The Amazing Cross*, p. 85)

 LIVING IT OUT

Becoming a Christian and being redeemed mean bringing every area of our lives into conformity to Christ and his commands. There is no halfway house and nothing is off limits. We are slaves of Christ 24/7, and he has purchaser's rights. As slaves of Christ we are chained to him and his commands: to love our neighbour, to be devoted to our marriage partner, to meditate on God's word, to tell others about Jesus, to be pure in our thought-life, to surrender our money and possessions to God. Being redeemed means we allow Christ mastery over every area of our lives.

(*The Amazing Cross*, p. 88)

8. Is there a particular area of your life that you need to submit or resubmit to Christ's control?

    • Your career

    • Your children

- Your health

- Your finances

- Your marriage

- Your future

The long, dull, monotonous years of middle-aged prosperity or middle-aged adversity are excellent campaigning weather for the devil.

(C. S. Lewis, *The Screwtape Letters*, p. 165

9. As we get older, it's easy to become weary of tackling sin. How can we spur each other on to keep living faithfully as slaves of God?

10. End this session by taking a look at the big picture. Redemption is not just an individual matter. The church is a community of people redeemed by God. How should this truth affect our:

- Behaviour towards church folk?

- Commitment to church this coming week?

▲ PRAYER TIME

If it's helpful, use the acronym **ACTS** to facilitate your prayers:

- **Adoration:** Worship God that he redeemed you; that Christ shed his blood to set you free from the penalty of sin.

- **Confession:** Ask forgiveness for the relationships, situations and issues you have not submitted to God's control.

- **Thanksgiving:** Thank God that Jesus is coming back soon to complete his work in us and take us to heaven.

- **Supplication:** Pray that people in your church would support one another, behaving like a redeemed community and pointing others to the truth of the gospel.

Your life is a journey you must travel with a deep consciousness of God. It cost God plenty to get you out of that dead-end, empty-headed life you grew up in. He paid with Christ's sacred blood, you know. He died like an unblemished, sacrificial lamb. And this was no afterthought. Even though it has only lately – at the end of the ages – become public knowledge, God always knew he was going to do this for you. It's because of this sacrificed Messiah, whom God then raised from the dead and glorified, that you trust God, that you know you have a future in God.

(1 Peter 1:18–21, *The Message*)

⬤ FURTHER STUDY

In 1 Corinthians 5:7 Paul describes Jesus as our Passover lamb. Read Exodus 12:1–30. How does the Passover feast point to Jesus' death on the cross?

SESSION 5

Reconciliation: Bridging the great divide

▶ INTRODUCTION

At the cross, the great divide between God and humanity was bridged. Jesus' sacrifice makes reconciliation with God possible: his enemies can now be his friends! But our own reconciliation with God is only the starting point: like a stone thrown into a pond, its effects should ripple out, affecting everyone around us. This is God's masterplan. The book of Revelation describes the scene in heaven where one day people of every tribe, language and nation will stand before God's throne. So how well are we doing? Why is church often full of people just like us? And how come, even among like-minded people, there is so much disunity? Perhaps we've made the message of reconciliation too much about ourselves, too much about our personal relationship with God? Perhaps it's time to redress the balance and see our reconciliation with God not as an end point, but as a catalyst, radically transforming our relationships with others.

READ *Ephesians 2:11-22*

[11] *Therefore, remember that formerly you who are Gentiles by birth and called 'uncircumcised' by those who call themselves 'the circumcision' (which is done in the body by human hands) –* [12] *remember that at that time you were separate from Christ, excluded from citizenship in Israel and foreigners to the covenants of the promise, without hope and without God in the world.* [13] *But now in Christ Jesus you who once were far away have been brought near by the blood of Christ.*

[14] *For he himself is our peace, who has made the two groups one and has destroyed the barrier, the dividing wall of hostility,* [15] *by setting aside in his flesh the law with its commands and regulations. His purpose was to create in himself one new humanity out of the two, thus making peace,* [16] *and in one body to reconcile both of them to God through the cross, by which he put to death their hostility.* [17] *He came and preached peace to you who were far away and peace to those who were near.* [18] *For through him we both have access to the Father by one Spirit.*

[19] *Consequently, you are no longer foreigners and strangers, but fellow citizens with God's people and also members of his household,* [20] *built on the foundation of the apostles and prophets, with Christ Jesus himself as the chief cornerstone.* [21] *In him the whole building is joined together and rises to become a holy temple in the Lord.* [22] *And in him you too are being built together to become a dwelling in which God lives by his Spirit.*

 ## FOCUS ON THE THEME

1. What divisions need reconciliation in the nation, in your local community and in the church?

◷ WHAT DOES THE BIBLE SAY?

2.   What were the reasons for the division between Jews and Gentiles?
     See verses 11–15.

3.   According to verses 14–18, what reconciliation did Jesus' death on
     the cross achieve?

4.   What is our reconciliation with other believers based on? See verses
     19–21.

5.   In verses 21–22 what images does Paul use to describe the church?
     What do these images tell us about the church's purpose and how it
     should function?

*The church is not a theological classroom. It is a conversion, confession,
repentance, reconciliation, forgiveness and sanctification centre, where
flawed people place their faith in Christ, gather to know and love him
better, and learn to love others as he designed.*

(Paul David Tripp, *Instruments in the Redeemer's Hands:
People in Need of Change Helping People in Need of Change*, p. 116)

◎ INVESTIGATE FURTHER

Read 2 Corinthians 5:16–21.

6.   How do we become Christ's ambassadors?

7.   Summarize the message of reconciliation in your own words.

♥ LIVING IT OUT

8.   How could you cross barriers in your church and encourage true community? Think about the activities you do and the relationships you are building with people, from:

- Different generations

- Different backgrounds

- Different Christian experience

- Different worship styles

Our reconciliation with others is the evidence that God has reconciled us to himself, the gospel is true and the Holy Spirit is at work in our lives.

(*The Amazing Cross*, p. 97)

9.	We want to make church as welcoming as possible for people, removing any barriers so they are not distracted from hearing the message of reconciliation. Try to view your church through the eyes of an unbeliever visiting for the first time:

•	Are there any obvious barriers to people hearing the gospel?

•	What changes could you make?

10.	Where do you meet people who need to be reconciled to God? What could you do to represent him better?

That is what your life is for; that God may make His appeal through you to the world.

(Eric Alexander, quoted in *The Amazing Cross*, p. 103)

▲ PRAYER TIME

Think about your sphere of influence and the places where you are Christ's ambassador. Are there five unbelievers you know whom you can pray for daily to become Christians? Pray for opportunities to share your faith with them.

● FURTHER STUDY

Read about the Council of Jerusalem in Acts 15. What was the disagreement about? What lessons can we learn from these godly men about how to seek reconciliation?

The fellowship of his suffering

▶ INTRODUCTION

Suffering is indiscriminate – it affects wealthy and poor, social high-flyers and those on benefits, devoted followers of Christ and atheists. There are no easy answers to why God allows suffering or how we should face it. But while it's a mystery, the cross stands against the backdrop of history, demonstrating that God knows about suffering because he himself suffered. Jesus hanging on the cross shatters the illusion that God is aloof. He loves us more than we could ever know - he understands our pain and stands with us in our suffering. And one of the great paradoxes of the Bible is that our suffering can actually have value. Suffering can stretch and prove our faith, bring us closer to God as we trust in him, and keep us looking forward to heaven.

Perhaps suffering could be what God uses to make you more like Jesus? As the nineteenth-century preacher Charles Spurgeon said, 'Many men [and women] owe the grandeur of their lives to their tremendous difficulties.'

READ *Mark 14:32-37, 43-46; 15:15-20, 31-34*

³²*They went to a place called Gethsemane, and Jesus said to his disciples, 'Sit here while I pray.' ³³He took Peter, James and John along with him, and he began to be deeply distressed and troubled. ³⁴'My soul is overwhelmed with sorrow to the point of death,' he said to them. 'Stay here and keep watch.'*

³⁵*Going a little farther, he fell to the ground and prayed that if possible the hour might pass from him. ³⁶'Abba, Father,' he said, 'everything is possible for you. Take this cup from me. Yet not what I will, but what you will.'*

³⁷*Then he returned to his disciples and found them sleeping. 'Simon,' he said to Peter, 'are you asleep? Couldn't you keep watch for one hour?*

⁴³*Just as he was speaking, Judas, one of the Twelve, appeared. With him was a crowd armed with swords and clubs, sent from the chief priests, the teachers of the law, and the elders.*

⁴⁴*Now the betrayer had arranged a signal with them: 'The one I kiss is the man; arrest him and lead him away under guard.' ⁴⁵Going at once to Jesus, Judas said, 'Rabbi!' and kissed him. ⁴⁶The men seized Jesus and arrested him.*

¹⁵*Wanting to satisfy the crowd, Pilate released Barabbas to them. He had Jesus flogged, and handed him over to be crucified.*

¹⁶*The soldiers led Jesus away into the palace (that is, the Praetorium) and called together the whole company of soldiers. ¹⁷They put a purple robe on him, then twisted together a crown of thorns and set it on him. ¹⁸And they began to call out to him, 'Hail, king of the Jews!' ¹⁹Again and again they struck him on the head with a staff and spat on him. Falling on their knees, they paid homage to him. ²⁰And when they had mocked him, they took off the purple robe and put his own clothes on him. Then they led him out to crucify him.*

³¹*The chief priests and the teachers of the law mocked him among themselves. 'He saved others,' they said, 'but he can't save himself!' ³²Let this Messiah, this king of Israel, come down now from the cross, that*

> we may see and believe.' Those crucified with him also heaped insults on him.
>
> [33]At noon, darkness came over the whole land until three in the afternoon. [34]And at three in the afternoon Jesus cried out in a loud voice, 'Eloi, Eloi, lema sabachthani?' (which means 'My God, my God, why have you forsaken me?').

 FOCUS ON THE THEME

1. Why does the issue of suffering have such a profound impact on Christians and non-Christians alike?

 WHAT DOES THE BIBLE SAY?

2. List all the ways Jesus suffered mentioned in these verses.

3. Look at verses 14:32–36. How did Jesus cope with suffering? What did he do?

4. What does this passage tell us about:

- How much God loves us?

- How much God understands about suffering?

I have turned ... to that lonely, twisted tortured figure on the cross, nails through hands and feet, back lacerated, limbs wrenched, brow bleeding from thorn pricks, mouth dry and intolerably thirsty, plunged in God-forsaken darkness. That is the God for me! He laid aside his immunity to pain. He entered our world of flesh and blood, tears and death. He suffered for us. Our sufferings become more manageable in light of his. There is still a question mark against human suffering, but over it we boldly stamp another mark, the cross which symbolizes divine suffering.

(John Stott, *The Cross of Christ*, p. 387)

◉ INVESTIGATE FURTHER

Read 1 Peter 1:3–9.

5. Look at verse 7. What positive results can come out of suffering?

6. According to this passage, in the midst of suffering:
- What do we have to look forward to?

- What should our attitude be?

Friends, when life gets really difficult, don't jump to the conclusion that God isn't on the job. Instead, be glad that you are in the very thick of what Christ experienced. This is a spiritual refining process, with glory just around the corner.

(1 Peter 4:12–13, The Message)

♥ LIVING IT OUT

7.   How would you respond in the following scenarios?

- A work colleague says, 'If your God is real, he would end suffering. Either he is not real or, worse than that, he just doesn't care about suffering.'

- A Christian friend tells you they have just been diagnosed with cancer.

8.   Reflect on 1 Peter 1:3–9. How should we pray when we, and other Christians, face suffering?

9.   Consider your own suffering – whether it's something you are going through at the moment, or something from your past:

- What do you think God is trying to teach you?

- How does reflecting on the cross help?

10.   This coming week, as you face various kinds of trials and suffering, which Bible truths will you cling to?

God takes us through afflictions in order to bring us to a recognition of our own helplessness, to bring our self-confidence to an end, and to teach us exclusive trust in God. In desperate times we learn to hold him fast.

(Jonathan Lamb, quoted in *The Amazing Cross*, p. 127)

▲ PRAYER TIME

- Pray for the struggles that each member of the group is facing.
- Ask that God would accomplish his purposes in our lives, making us more like Christ.
- Focus on our hope of heaven – when Christ's glory will be seen and our suffering is finally over.

Keep a cool head. Stay alert. The Devil is poised to pounce, and would like nothing better than to catch you napping. Keep your guard up. You're not the only ones plunged into these hard times. It's the same with Christians all over the world. So keep a firm grip on the faith. The suffering won't last forever. It won't be long before this generous God who has great plans for us in Christ – eternal and glorious plans they are! – will have you put together and on your feet for good. He gets the last word; yes, he does.

(1 Peter 5:8–11, *The Message*)

● FURTHER STUDY

Find out how God has used suffering in the lives of other Christians. There are many excellent Christian biographies available. Below is a small sample:

Faith Cook, *Stars in God's Sky* (Evangelical Press, 2009)
Eric Metaxas, *Seven Men: And the Secret of Their Greatness* (Thomas Nelson, 2013)
Eric Metaxas, *Seven Women: And the Secret of Their Greatness* (Thomas Nelson, 2015)
Andrew and Rachel Wilson, *The Life You Never Expected: Thriving while Parenting Special Needs Children* (IVP, 2015)

Notes for leaders

As a leader, your role is not to answer every question, but to facilitate group discussion and to help people focus on what God's Word says. Ensure that you make time during the week to read the Bible passages and questions. Look at the Notes for leaders and see how best to present the questions and generate discussion.

In order to make the most of your group time, it is a great help if each member can read the passage and think about the subject of the study in advance. Of course, this is difficult when members don't have much time to sit down and prepare.

Don't rush through the study; feel free to miss out some questions and focus on what's most pertinent to your group. The aim is not just to learn about the issues under discussion, but to see how they impact our life and are foundational to our faith.

Be aware of the group dynamics. Some people are eager to contribute, and others less so. You may have to encourage quieter folk to participate, and ask the more vocal ones to listen! Invite a number of replies to each question so that people can share what they have prepared and learn from one another's responses.

It is important to leave time at the end of the session for prayer and to sum up what God has taught you. Make sure that group members go home clear about the main message of the study and how they are going to apply it in their lives in the coming week.

Your group may be well established and your members prepared to talk at a deep level. New groups may take time to settle. However, as your group members get to know one another, you'll not just be talking about the issues, but developing a true sense of Christian community as you pray, share, learn and grow together.

This study guide stands alone. However, it is based on the book *The Amazing Cross* (IVP, 2012). Group members and leaders may find it helpful to read the relevant chapters as a companion to the study guide. The book can be purchased or downloaded from www.ivpbooks.com.

SESSION 1

1. When we face difficult circumstances or God doesn't seem to be answering our prayers, it is tempting to conclude that he doesn't love us. Despite what the Bible teaches about believers suffering, about carrying our cross, and the consequences of living in a fallen world, we still hope that God will prove his love to us by making us happy and improving our lives.

2. God demonstrates his love for us in many ways, but Paul mentions two here. From the moment we become Christians, the Holy Spirit pours God's love into our hearts so that we have assurance that we are his dearly loved children (verse 5). The Father also showed his love by sending his Son to die for us – an objective, one-time event (verse 8).

3. Jesus died for us when we were God's enemies – we were neither righteous nor good. Even though our sin was abhorrent to God and there was nothing lovely about us, he took the initiative to restore the relationship, and so demonstrated his lavish love.

4. God's love in our hearts is like a deposit or down payment. It is a guarantee so that we can be confident in our hope of heaven. We can be sure that God will finish our sanctification; our transformation will one day be complete.

5. Difficult circumstances and suffering do not indicate that God doesn't love us. In fact, according to these verses we can rejoice and continue to trust God's love for us because he gives purpose to our suffering. God uses hardships and difficult circumstances to develop a Christ-like character in us and to keep us focused on heaven.

6. • Psalm 23:1–4: God provides guidance; he leads us and is with us in every circumstance. He provides security, comfort, restoration and peace for our souls.

   • Matthew 5:43–45: God shows his love impartially – he sends rain and sun on all. He sustains all life and makes it flourish.

- Romans 8:34: Jesus is daily interceding for us.

- Hebrews 12:5–6: God shows his love for us by disciplining us.

7. Reflect on Jesus' life and his death at Calvary. Every day Jesus listened to God, obeyed his will, sought to give him glory, prayed to him and encouraged others to seek him. Jesus demonstrated his love for his Father by laying aside his glory and making the Father's will his own. Ask for the Holy Spirit's help as we follow Jesus' example of listening to God, obeying him, denying our own preferences and priorities, and choosing God's will instead.

8. Be creative! Here are just a few examples. We could demonstrate God's self-giving love by being willing to serve one another practically; not holding on tightly to our own preferences, but instead being willing to make sacrifices for the sake of others; and seeking to honour and esteem others rather than ourselves. For example, it could mean inviting another family round for a meal; keeping silent about our own preferences so that someone else's needs are met; promoting the gifts of others in your church rather than your own.

9. We need to listen well as our friends and colleagues share their thoughts and feelings. Seek to offer encouragement, kindness and support. We don't need to share all that we believe in a single conversation. But occasionally, there are genuine opportunities to share what the Bible teaches.

- Encourage your Christian friends to reflect on all the daily demonstrations of God's love. Point them back to the cross where God clearly showed his love. Challenge them that suffering doesn't disprove God's love, but is an opportunity to grow in Christ-likeness. Pray with them that they wouldn't believe the devil's lies, but would trust God's good purposes even when they can't see his hand.

- Explain that much of the evil that happens does so because we have free will and humans make wrong choices. If God took away our free will, then we would be robots, incapable of wrong but also incapable of love and devotion. Rather than condone evil, in the death of Jesus God took the initiative to defeat evil once and for all. This victory will be seen when Jesus returns to earth. Meanwhile, the days of evil are limited.

- Jesus' death on the cross was barbaric, but God sent his only Son to die because he loved us so much. And Jesus died willingly because he knew that there was no other way to satisfy the righteous wrath of the Trinity. The penalty for our sin was death, and only Jesus' death could satisfy God's righteous requirements. God sent his Son to die in our place so that we wouldn't have to, so that our relationship with him would be restored.

10. If we were aware of how very much God loved us, we would know an inner peace and joy, regardless of our circumstances. We would be secure, not having to compete for anyone else's love or attention, because we had God's. We would be quick to forgive others, knowing how much we had been forgiven.

    Spend time each day meditating on God's love – worship him for all his daily gifts and benefits, and reflect on the cross and the love demonstrated there.

SESSION 2

1. It is easier to live with a lopsided view of God – where his love far exceeds his wrath. This is partly because we don't realize how serious and offensive our sin is to God, and partly because we imagine ourselves losing our temper, lashing out in anger, and we can't believe God is like that. He's not! God's wrath is his just and righteous abhorrence of sin because he is absolutely holy. His wrath is a measure of his white-hot holiness.

2. We are like sheep wandering in the field without a shepherd. Sin is doing our own thing (however good it seems) without any thought of God. It is a total disregard for God, his laws and his values.

3. Some suggested phrases you could pick out:

   - Facing God's wrath: 'we considered him punished by God, stricken by him, and afflicted' (verse 4); 'yet it was the LORD's will to crush him and cause him to suffer' (verse 10).

   - Taking our punishment: 'He was pierced for our transgressions, he was crushed for our iniquities; the punishment that brought us peace was on him, and by his wounds we are healed' (verse 5); 'the LORD has laid on him the iniquity of us all' (verse 6); 'for the transgression of my people he was stricken' (verse 8); 'the LORD makes his life an offering for sin' (verse 10).

4. God hates sin so much that he was willing to go to extreme measures to defeat it. Isaiah describes how God allowed his only Son to die in our place to pay the punishment for our sin. The prophet describes in excruciating detail the agony Christ went through on the cross. He was 'crushed' (verses 5 and 10). Isaiah also repeats graphic words like 'punishment', 'affliction' and 'transgression'.

5. God wanted his people to know that Jesus' death was not an accident or an aberration, but was critical to his plan of salvation; that Jesus willingly submitted to the cross; that finally, after all the other sacrifices for sin, Jesus' death was a once-and-for-all sacrifice.

6. Hebrews 7:26–28: Jesus was able to appease God's wrath because he was the perfect sacrifice. Other priests had to offer sacrifices for their own sins, but because Jesus was sinless, he was able to die in our place. Because he was sinless, his death was a once-and-for-all event.

7. Because of Christ's death, we do not face the penalty of our sin; our salvation is not in dispute. However, there will be a day of reckoning for believers:

   • We will all appear before God's judgment seat to give an account of how we have lived as believers (2 Corinthians 5:10).

   • As Christians, it is possible to build on the foundation of the gospel with wood, hay and stubble: worthless service for Christ that will not stand up to God's scrutiny. It is also possible to build with precious stones – faithful service based on the Word of God – and have a legacy that will last for eternity. Depending on how we live as believers, some of us will get to heaven 'by the skin of our teeth' (1 Corinthians 3:12–15)!

8. Be gracious in your conversations, sharing God's truth with love.

   • We tend to excuse the sins we commit as acceptable! But the goal is not to excuse and justify our sin, or indeed to grade it according to our warped sinful perspective. All sin demonstrates rebellion against God, and that in itself is serious. The aim is to tackle and root out sin in our lives ruthlessly (Ephesians 4:17–31; Colossians 3:1–17).

   • Romans 3:23–26: we have all sinned; none of our achievements or good living can make us right before God. We could never attain God's perfect standard of holiness. The only way for our relationship with God to be restored, the only way for us to be sure of an eternal home in heaven, is to trust in Jesus' death on the cross – he died in our place, a perfect sacrifice, able to satisfy God's demand for justice and pay the penalty for our sin.

9. We acknowledge God has forgiven our sins, but often we struggle to really believe it. This can lead to endless service for God in the hope

that our good deeds will impress him, or we may avoid serving him as we feel unworthy. Guilt can rob us of the peace and joy of our salvation, as we are never quite sure that God could really love us.

We can only get rid of guilt when we acknowledge that Christ's sacrifice on Calvary was sufficient to pay the price for our sin. Jesus' death dealt with our sin decisively and completely. When we are racked with guilt, we need to come back to Jesus' cross – to realize what was accomplished there and the freedom Christ won for us (Romans 8:1). If we give in to guilt, we are giving Satan another victory.

10. Encourage group members to be specific and think how they are going to stay motivated to live for God this week. What practical steps are needed to keep focused?

SESSION 3

1. Share examples of when someone showed you undeserved kindness. Perhaps someone brought a meal round to your home for no reason other than kindness. Perhaps they babysat your children so you could have a night out. You may come up with lots of examples of grace or you may discover that showing grace is not very common in your family and sphere of influence. If so, what can you do to inspire people to show more grace?

2. 'No' is repeated again and again to underscore that no-one is righteous in God's sight. No-one's goodness can compare to God's standard of righteousness. It doesn't matter whether you are a Jew or a Gentile, or how much of God's law you have tried to keep – we are all sinners in his sight. 'All' is repeated in order to highlight that a way back to God is available to everyone. Everyone who believes will be justified. Regardless of our background or our past sin, God's grace justifies us all.

3. Jesus died to save us. Justification is based solely on Jesus' death on the cross (verses 24–25). It was a legal transaction: Jesus paid the penalty for my sin, and the result is that I am justified in God's sight. When we are justified, two things happen. Jesus takes our sin, but he also gives us his righteousness (verses 20, 22). We receive a declaration of righteousness from God. Of course, we still sin, but when God looks on us, he no longer sees our sin; he sees Christ's righteousness. We can do nothing to justify ourselves. Justification is a free gift, an act of god's grace (verse 24). All we can do is put our faith and trust in what Jesus' death accomplished for us on the cross (verses 22, 25).

4. Keeping the law or doing good works can't affect whether or not we are justified before God (verse 20). There is no way we could keep all of the law all the time, or do enough good works to reach God's standard of holiness.

   Similarly, our justification is not based on our achievements after we have become a Christian, nor is it put in jeopardy by our sins. Our justification is based solely on Christ's achievements at Calvary. There is nothing we can do to add to, or take away from, our justification.

5. God is holy, he does not lower his standard of holiness and he cannot tolerate sin. His justice demands that sin is punished and his wrath is appeased. But he is also full of love. God knew that there was nothing we could do to save ourselves and that we needed to be rescued from sin. He took the initiative to make a plan of salvation – God the Father sent his only Son to die in our place. This verse helps us appreciate the love, holiness and righteousness of God.

6. Justification means we have peace with God – this is not primarily a subjective feeling, but an objective status. Our relationship with God is restored, and we are no longer God's enemies, but his friends. We are now living in the sphere of God's grace – recipients of his daily kindness, enjoying an intimate relationship with him. We can also be confident of heaven, when we will see and share in God's glory.

7. Knowing that he has received a righteousness from God doesn't make Paul complacent. He is keen to sacrifice everything else in order to have a life centred on Christ. He wants a relationship with Christ that is personal, growing, life transforming and powerful. He wants to identify with Christ, even in his suffering, and he looks forward to heaven with great anticipation.

8. • It is helpful to tell new Christians that justification is an objective truth: it refers to our legal standing before God. How we feel about God may change depending on our circumstances – we may feel elated in a worship service, but glum as we go to work on Monday. Thankfully, our salvation does not depend on our feelings; it depends on Christ's death on the cross.

    • We feel grieved that God could forgive people who seem more sinful than us. But that is largely because we are viewing sin from our own perspective. We need to see all sin as abhorrent to a holy God. When we see all sin as God sees it, we are glad that he forgives the 'big' sins, because that means he can forgive me – nothing and no-one is outside the scope of his salvation.

- We may have to deal with the consequences of past sins, but justification means that our punishment has already been meted out on Christ. He has paid for our sins. None of the difficulties we face is a result of God being vindictive.

9. Recognizing our justification is based on what Christ has done for us means that we can be secure in, and sure of, our salvation, regardless of how we feel or how good our day has been. Our salvation is not dependent on our good behaviour, whether God feels near or life is going well. Because justification is based on Christ's sacrifice, there is no room for boasting, no point in comparing ourselves with other believers, no need to believe the devil's lies about our guilt.

10. Grace may be demonstrated in forgiving others, not holding a grudge, and giving each other the benefit of the doubt. There are countless different ways to show it, for example, in our active support of young people learning to lead in church, or in our efforts to develop and be involved in projects for the local community.

SESSION 4

1. If we acknowledge that we were born in sin, we recognize sin as part of our DNA. We know we are enslaved by sin and need someone else to rescue us. If, however, we believe we were born good, we assume we just need to create a good environment and we will continue to be good. We trust in our own righteousness and our own efforts, and don't look for a saviour.

2. Animal sacrifices could cleanse people only outwardly and temporarily. Jesus' sacrifice was a once-and-for-all event. Because he was sinless, he was able to die in our place, paying the penalty for sin and cleansing us completely.

3. We are not just superficially clean; we are cleansed to the core of our being, cleansed from our failure to keep God's law (verses 14–15). We are now able to serve God and please him, rather than having to serve sin and the devil (verse 14). We have now received our eternal inheritance – a relationship with Christ and an eternal home in heaven with our Father (verse 15).

4. High priests had to keep repeating their sacrifices, because they used the blood of animals which cleansed the people only temporarily. Jesus' sacrifice was better because he was sinless. His death was able perfectly to satisfy God's wrath once and for all.

5. Jesus is now in heaven interceding for us, praying for us and pleading our case before his Father (see also Hebrews 7:25). He is waiting to return to earth a second time, to complete our salvation and take us home to heaven.

6. At the cross Jesus bought our freedom. His blood paid the ransom for our sin, set us free from Satan's grasp and delivered us into God's kingdom where we are free to serve him. We changed from being slaves to sin to being slaves of God. Satan no longer holds us captive to sin. Although Satan's power is still evident in our world, we don't have to obey him. In the Holy Spirit's power we are able to live righteously.

7. 'Counting ourselves dead to sin … does not mean pretending that sin does not exist or that we are perfect, but acknowledging that through Jesus' death on the cross our debt to sin has been paid, the law has been satisfied, Satan's claim on us is over, the bonds of sin have been broken, we have a new master and are free to live a new life in Christ' (*The Amazing Cross*, p. 85). We mustn't let sin have free reign in our bodies. So we don't excuse or ignore sin, but with the Holy Spirit's power, we tackle it and root it out wherever we see it growing in our lives. However, holy living is not just saying 'no to sin'; Paul says we must offer ourselves to God. We must take positive action, giving ourselves wholeheartedly to Christ's service.

8. Use the quote above this question in the 'Living it out' section to generate discussion. Encourage the group to be specific about the sins they need to deal with.

9. Tackling sin is exhausting. It is easier to hide secret sins, or excuse them as part of our personality. Discuss ways in which you can support one other. For example, if you aren't already in a prayer triplet or accountability group, organize this.

10. If we keep remembering that every believer is a blood-bought member of Christ's family, we will be more eager to forgive, esteem, look after and take a practical and personal interest in one another. If we regard all believers as 'precious in God's sight', we are more likely to treat them accordingly. This truth should also help to motivate us to invest our time, money and energy in our church community.

SESSION 5

1. As appropriate, be honest about the racial, economic, theological, educational, social and gender divisions in your church, community and nation.

2. Paul explains that the Jews and Gentiles were divided over the issue of circumcision. The law was an issue of contention between the two groups. The Gentiles did not observe the law, and the Jews felt that they obeyed it perfectly. Both groups had a different understanding of how to please God.

3. Jesus' death meant that both Jews and Gentiles could be reconciled to God, as well as to each other.

4. Reconciliation with other believers is not based on lofty ideals or emotional hype. Our unity together is based on the work of Christ on the cross. God's Word, which contains the teachings of the apostles and prophets, also forms the foundation upon which we can work together.

5. Paul describes the church as a building and a temple. As a building, the church is constantly under construction, dynamically growing and developing. The image of the temple reminds us of the role of the church – we exist to worship and glorify God. The Holy Spirit lives and operates in the corporate body of the church, not just within individuals.

6. As soon as we are reconciled to God, as soon as we are 'in Christ' (verse 13), we become Christ's ambassadors. Sharing and living out the gospel is not just for paid ministers or super-spiritual Christians. Each believer is given this ministry of reconciliation to share with others.

7. Encourage the group to come up with a few ways to explain the gospel succinctly. What are the main points that have to be included? What is superfluous?

8. Encourage the group to make specific suggestions. For example, a younger person could ask an older Christian to mentor them; each week a different group member could share about their background and how they became a Christian; you could use a variety of worship styles in your small group – liturgy, for example, or praying simultaneously like the Koreans do!

9. Think about issues such as: Are there enough seats set out? Does everyone have their own special seat, or can you sit anywhere? Are people welcomed warmly as they come into the church? Are visitors spoken to afterwards? Are the crèche and other facilities labelled properly? It is useful to think through these issues carefully, because sometimes small changes can make a huge difference to someone's experience of church.

10. Encourage group members to consider their daily routine and the variety of people in their sphere of influence. Think about the impression of God and the gospel people receive from watching your life.

SESSION 6

1. Both Christians and non-Christians wrestle with the issue of suffering, because it is a mystery. It can't be predicted, avoided or shared. Those who believe there is a God struggle to grasp why he would allow suffering, and non-Christians often use this as a reason not to believe.

2. Jesus suffered physically, emotionally, spiritually. He was betrayed by his friends, forsaken by his Father, mocked by soldiers and religious leaders, flogged and spat upon, and he endured the crown of thorns and the cross. We can only imagine the disappointment, loneliness and agony he endured. He can identify with our suffering because he himself suffered.

3. Jesus prayed and brought his situation before God; he surrounded himself with good friends (even though they fell asleep!); and he submitted himself to God's will, regardless of how his prayers would be answered.

4. This scene reminds us how much God loves us and the lengths to which he was willing to go in order to restore our relationship with him: he sent his only Son to die in our place; he allowed all the sin of the world – past, present and future – to be laid on him, and for the first time ever the fellowship of the Trinity was broken, as God could no longer look upon Jesus.

    God is not distant or remote from suffering. Both the Father and Son suffered to save us. God knows that Jesus' suffering on the cross was necessary in order to fulfil his good purposes for us. He assessed that the pain of Christ's suffering was worth it to save us. Perhaps this points to the truth that sometimes God allows suffering, because it is the only way his perfect will can be achieved.

5. Suffering can refine our faith and prove it is genuine. Sometimes the reality of our faith and our trust in God can be proved only when trials cause us to reassess our priorities and reveal who and what we are depending on. This kind of pure faith will mean greater praise, glory and honour for Jesus when he returns to earth for the second time.

6. We can look forward to our own resurrection from the dead, our eternal inheritance as God's children, and our home in heaven. Our attitude should be one of praise for our salvation and all the eternal blessings God has given us. We can also be joyful, not for our suffering, but in our suffering, because we know how God's salvation story will end. We know that our suffering is momentary compared to the everlasting joys of heaven.

7. Suffering is a challenging issue to talk to people about, because it is personal and they are hurting. We cannot claim to know all the answers, and sometimes a hug or a meal delivered to a friend dealing with tragedy are more effective than any words we can say. Perhaps you could explain to your work colleague that we don't know why God does not put an end to suffering, but we do know that he cares about it. He joined us in our suffering, so he understands. His Son suffered on the cross to defeat sin, so, ultimately, if we trust him, our suffering will be over. When talking with a friend who has been diagnosed with an illness, be careful not to come up with answers and reasons for their predicament, as Job's friends did. Comfort them, pray with them for healing and for God's will to be done. In your conversations help them to turn their eyes to God for strength and comfort.

8. Pray that we would be conscious of God's mercy to us, that we would keep our eyes on our eternal blessings and our home in heaven. Pray that, regardless of the circumstances, we would be joyful because we know God is sanctifying us and we are looking forward to Jesus' return. Pray that God would use this suffering to refine our faith, mature us and teach us all he wants us to learn. Pray that in all of life's circumstances we would be faithful witnesses for him.

9. Help group members to think through their suffering and what God may be trying to teach them. Focus on the cross, remembering: our salvation which is secure regardless of our circumstances; God's understanding of, and presence in, our pain; the mysterious way God works out his purposes through our suffering; our home in heaven.

10. Reflect on the passages you have looked at in this study. Is there a particular verse or Bible truth you can cling to this week?

Resources

Oswald Chambers, *My Utmost for His Highest* (Discovery House, 2014)

Tim Chester, *Mission Matters: Love Says Go* (IVP, 2015)

Tim Chester, *The Ordinary Hero: Living the Cross and Resurrection* (IVP, 2009)

Brian Edwards and Ian Shaw, *The Divine Substitute: The Atonement in the Bible and History* (Day One Publications, 2006)

Steve Jeffery, Mike Ovey and Andrew Sach, *Pierced for Our Transgressions: Rediscovering the Glory of Penal Substitution* (IVP, 2007)

Timothy Keller, *The Reason for God: Belief in an Age of Scepticism* (Hodder & Stoughton, 2009)

Timothy Keller, *King's Cross: The Story of the World in the Life of Jesus* (Hodder & Stoughton, 2013)

C. S. Lewis, *The Screwtape Letters* (HarperOne, 2013)

John R. W. Stott, *The Cross of Christ* (IVP, 1986)

John R. W. Stott, *The Message of Romans* (IVP, 1994)

Steve Timmis, *I Wish Jesus Hadn't Said That . . . But I'm Really Glad He Did!* (IVP, 2013)

Paul David Tripp, *Instruments in the Redeemer's Hands: People in Need of Change Helping People in Need of Change* (P & R, 2002)

Keswick Ministries

Our purpose

Keswick Ministries is committed to the spiritual renewal of God's people for his mission in the world.

God's purpose is to bring his blessing to all the nations of the world. That promise of blessing, which touches every aspect of human life, is ultimately fulfilled through the life, death, resurrection, ascension and future return of Christ. All of the people of God are called to participate in his missionary purposes, wherever he may place them. The central vision of *Keswick Ministries* is to see the people of God equipped, encouraged and refreshed to fulfil that calling, directed and guided by God's Word in the power of his Spirit, for the glory of his Son.

Our priorities

Keswick Ministries seeks to serve the local church through:

- **Hearing God's Word**: the Scriptures are the foundation for the church's life, growth and mission, and *Keswick Ministries* is committed to preach and teach God's Word in a way that is faithful to Scripture and relevant to Christians of all ages and backgrounds.

- **Becoming like God's Son**: from its earliest days the Keswick movement has encouraged Christians to live godly lives in the power of the Spirit, to grow in Christ-likeness and to live under his lordship in every area of life. This is God's will for his people in every culture and generation.

- **Serving God's mission**: the authentic response to God's Word is obedience to his mission, and the inevitable result of Christ-likeness is sacrificial service. *Keswick Ministries* seeks to encourage committed discipleship in family life, work and society, and energetic engagement in the cause of world mission.

Our ministry

- **Keswick: the event**. Every summer the town of Keswick hosts a three-week Convention, which attracts some 15,000 Christians from the UK and around the world. The event provides Bible teaching for all ages, vibrant worship, a sense of unity across generations and denominations, and an inspirational call to serve Christ in the world. It caters for children of all ages and has a strong youth and young adult programme. And it all takes place in the beautiful Lake District – a perfect setting for rest, recreation and refreshment.

- **Keswick: the movement**. For 140 years the work of Keswick has impacted churches worldwide, and today the movement is underway throughout the UK, as well as in many parts of Europe, Asia, North America, Australia, Africa and the Caribbean. *Keswick Ministries* is committed to strengthen the network in the UK and beyond, through prayer, news, pioneering and cooperative activity.

- **Keswick resources**. *Keswick Ministries* is producing a growing range of books and booklets based on the core foundations of Christian life and mission. It makes Bible teaching available through free access to mp3 downloads, and the sale of DVDs and CDs. It broadcasts online through Clayton TV and annual BBC Radio 4 services. In addition to the summer Convention, Keswick Ministries is hoping to develop other teaching and training events in the coming years.

Our unity

The Keswick movement worldwide has adopted a key Pauline statement to describe its gospel inclusivity: 'for you are all one in Christ Jesus' (Galatians 3:28). *Keswick Ministries* works with evangelicals from a wide variety of church backgrounds, on the understanding that they share a commitment to the essential truths of the Christian faith as set out in our statement of belief.

Our contact details

T: 017687 80075   *E*: info@keswickministries.org
W: www: keswickministries.org
Mail: Keswick Ministries, Keswick Convention Centre, Skiddaw Street, Keswick, CA12 4BY England

also by Elizabeth McQuoid

The Amazing Cross
Transforming lives today
Jeremy & Elizabeth McQuoid

ISBN: 978-1-84474-587-6
192 pages, paperback

The cross of Christ is the heartbeat of Christianity. It is a place of pain and horror, wonder and beauty, all at the same time. It is the place where our sin collided gloriously with God's grace.

But do we really understand what the cross is all about? Or are we so caught up in the peripherals of the faith that we have forgotten the core? We need to ask ourselves:

• How deep an impact has the cross made on my personality?
• Do I live in the light of the freedom it has won for me?
• Am I dying to myself every day, so that I can live for Christ?
• Do I face suffering with faith and assurance?
• Can I face death in the light of the hope of the resurrection?

The authors present us with a contemporary challenge to place all of our lives, every thought, word and deed, under the shadow of the amazing cross, and allow that cross to transform us here and now.

'It is an ideal introduction to the heart of the Christian gospel, and a very welcome addition to the Keswick Foundation series.' Jonathan Lamb

Available from your local Christian bookshop or **www.ivpbooks.com**

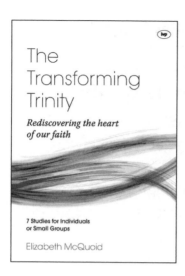

The
Transforming
Trinity
*Rediscovering the heart
of our faith*

7 Studies for Individuals
or Small Groups

Elizabeth McQuoid

also by Elizabeth McQuoid

KESWICK STUDY GUIDE

The Transforming Trinity

*Rediscovering the heart
of our faith*
Elizabeth McQuoid

ISBN: 978-1-84474-906-5
80 pages, booklet

Does believing in the Trinity make any difference in real life?

These seven studies will help you grow in your understanding of the inexhaustible riches of the Trinity. Find out why the Trinity is central to our beliefs and fundamental to the working out of our faith.

Learn to worship the triune God more fully, reflect his image more clearly, and experience his transforming power in your life. Learn what it really means to know the Father, follow the Son, and walk in the Spirit.

Because the Trinity is at the heart of Christian faith and life.

'Encounter and be transformed by the living God, Father, Son and Spirit. Highly recommended!' Dr Steve Brady

'Will help you explore this wonderful theme, engaging your heart, stretching your mind and changing your life!' John Risbridger

'A feast for individuals and Bible study groups.' Sam Allberry

---

Available from your local Christian bookshop or **www.ivpbooks.com**

related titles from IVP

KESWICK STUDY GUIDE 2015

The Whole of Life for Christ

Becoming everyday disciples

Antony Billington
& Mark Greene

ISBN: 978-1-78359-361-3
96 pages, booklet

Suppose for a moment that Jesus really is interested in every aspect of your life. Everything - the dishes and the dog and the day job and the drudgery of some of the stuff you just have to do, the TV programme you love, the staff in your local supermarket as well as the homeless in the local shelter, your boss as well as your vicar, helping a shopper find the ketchup as well as brewing the tea for the life group, the well-being of your town and the well-being of your neighbour ...

Suppose the truth that every Christian is a new creature in Christ, empowered by the Spirit to do his will, means that Christ is with you everywhere you go, in every task you do, with every person you meet ... Suppose God wants to involve you in what he's doing in the places you spend your time day by day ... Suppose your whole life is important to Christ ...

He does.

These seven studies will help you explore and live out the marvellous truth that the gospel is an invitation into whole-life discipleship, into a life following and imitating Jesus.

Available from your local Christian bookshop or **www.ivpbooks.com**